The Lord be with
you always.

Love ya
Ashley

Contents

Acknowledgements

I would like to give thanks to God for giving me this gift to write.

Thanks for the sincere encouragement from my family and friends.

I give special thanks to my dear friend and confidant, "Joey" and

the inspiration of his life that brought this book into fruition.

3

Introduction

Joey "Another Joseph"

One of the greatest and much beloved stories in the Bible is that of the story of Joseph, *the boy with the coat of many colors:* (Genesis chapter 37 through chapters 49). The intrigue of the story is not about the coat of many colors; it is about a young boy and his dreams about becoming a leader. Joseph's dreams were crushed beneath the feet of ignorance and jealousy displayed by his brothers after he shared his dreams with them. Joseph's brothers were filled with so much indignation that they staged a mock murder and put him in a pit to die. Later, the decision was made to sell him to a band of Midianite merchantmen and they, in return, took him into Egypt and sold him into slavery.

I am quite sure that it appeared to Joseph that his end was near. But you see; *all of his days had not come in.* After Joseph's days had come in, he was exalted from being a slave to a slave master. The story of Joey, another Joseph, is similar to that of Joseph. Joey is young man born into a large twentieth century family of eight, who also dreamed of becoming a great leader someday. But, just like Joseph, Joey made an attempt to share his dreams and even his personal struggles with his siblings. Because of this, Joey dreams were shattered. They did not lower him into a pit, nor did they stage a mock death for Joey. But their rejection of him was

4

so great, that to Joey, life felt like an open abyss. So feeling like he was no longer loved, and possibly feeling as though he was at the end of his rope, Joey's life took a roller coaster ride on a quest in search of love in all of the wrong places. Finding love in all the wrong places actually led to a type of enslavement for Joey. Oh yes, it looked like this was the end for Joey, but you see, *all of his days had not come in.* For after all of his days had come in, he also ended up being a great leader, with enough love and compassion to reach back and lend a helping hand to his siblings. A word to the wise: *Do not make permanent decisions based on temporary circumstances.* Just wait until enough days have come in. Then make an intelligent assessment of your situation. You will see a greater manifestation of who you were born to be from your mother's womb <u>and</u> the destiny that awaits you.

Chapter 1

"The Coat of Many Colors"

Joey, a twentieth century teenager, was raised in the concrete jungle of one of America's largest cities, Washington, D.C. As a child growing up with his eight siblings, Joey was always favored and loved by his Father very much. Joey's Father loved him so much that he also gave him a coat of many colors. It wasn't a coat that Joey could wear to protect himself from the wind's chill. However, Joey was cloaked with the favor of his father in many ways. He was a multi-talented kid. Joey was an artist from his birth. He could take a number-two pencil and a sheet of plain white paper and draw whatever image would come into his head. He entered his drawings many times in contests that were given by his school's art department. Joey's drawings always won first place but by the time he had reached the eighth grade, his dreams of being an artist were shattered by the jealousy of one of his brothers who deliberately hid his drawing kit and drawings. By the time they were found, Joey had lost all interest in art and began pursuing another one of his many talents.

There was no child or adult, living in Salley Whitlock Housing Project who could write like Joey could write. First of all, he was a lefty. This made most people scratch their head and say, *"how can a left hand person write this well?"* Nevertheless, Joey made quite a reputation for himself writing love letters and poems for the local teenage sweethearts. Joey perfected his penmanship by sitting at the kitchen table, hours upon hours writing and re-writing, until he had become the master of any pen or pencil that came in contact with his left hand. His love for good or perfect penmanship gave him many dreams of becoming a writer or editor of some book company. The dream was crushed when all of the other boys in the project started calling him names and referring to his perfect penmanship as a sign of being a sissy. As we all know, the opinions of others can sometimes make or break us, especially if we are a person wrestling with low self-esteem. Well in Joey's case, the opinions of others did have a way of hurting him and destroying his dreams. Nevertheless, Joey had a way of taking every hurt, every crushing word and using them as stepping-stones to take him from one day to the next. The more attacks that Joey suffered from his siblings and neighborhood playmates, the more his Father esteemed him better than all of the rest. His Father was the only one who never stopped loving him. As a matter of fact let me take a few moments to introduce you to Joey's loving father. Joey's father is the same father of Joseph of the Bible.

God Almighty.

Chapter 2

"Sold into Slavery"

Though many would speak love, few were willing to show love to little Joey. Living in the ghetto had its burdens and sorrows that at times were hard to bear. Even the love of his mother was not strong enough to soothe Joey's hurts.

Shelia was her name. At one time, Shelia was the prettiest young woman that ever lived in the Whitlock Projects. But after many years of struggling, living on welfare and living in an abusive relationship, she now bore the scars and attitude of a very deprived woman. Shelia raised her eight children the best that she knew how. The greatest mistake that she may have made was not allowing her children to get to know their heavenly Father, as they should have. But then, it was the only way that she knew. She did not get acquainted with her Father until she was a grown woman with eight adult children. She has since struggled to maintain a good relationship with Him: a woman with giving hands, but a closed heart.

It was at the tender age of thirteen that Joey and one of his younger sisters would hang out at the local supermarket on Saturdays to pick up some change from shoppers who needed help carrying their groceries. It was on one particular Saturday afternoon that the two of them had just decided to call it a day. They had been helping neighborhood people carry their groceries all day long. Their little pockets were just about bursting with change. Though tired, they were anxious to get home to count up their day's earning. As they started walking home, a friendly-faced, chubby little man wearing crisp and clean smelling clothes approached them. He enlisted their services to help him carry his groceries to his car, which was parked just around the corner. As tired as they were, after this little man had flashed a five-dollar bill in their face several times, it was not a hard decision to make. By the time they all made it to his car, this little chubby man had introduced himself as Bob and had asked them their names.

"I'm Joey, and this is my sister Ellen."

"Well Joey and Ellen," Bob said, as he gave them a great big smile of gratitude. "I really appreciate your help. Here is the five dollars that I promised you. By the way, if you kids would like I will give you a lift to your house. All you have to do is just tell me where you live."

Joey turned and looked at Ellen, and then replied, "No thanks, we live really close to here."

"So do I," said Bob. "I live about two more blocks in that direction," Bob said pointing, "Just past the projects."

"That's just by where we live!" shouted Ellen.

"Well then hop in, and I'll take you there. And I won't take no for an answer."

So they all got in the nice big Buick and rode home. As they were pulling onto the street they lived on, Shelia was sitting outside on the stoop waiting for her children to come home. She recognized them getting out of the car.   So she stood up and walked over to the car with a look of disgust on her face. As soon as he had stopped the car, Bob got out, introduced himself and attempted to explain to Shelia how and why her two children were with a total stranger. Shelia, feeling a bit less stressed, thanked Bob for giving the children a ride.

"No problem," Bob replied. "As a matter of fact, if it's alright with you, I would like to hire little Joey to help me with a few chores some Saturdays. I will pay him whatever you and he decide to charge…that is if he is interested as well."

"Well, I don't know. We will have to talk this over. I guess, if he is interested, it will be alright with me," said Shelia.

9

"Well, here is my telephone number, if you should decide just give me a call."

"Thanks."

The next few days Shelia spent talking with her neighbors about this trendy little rich popper who was so nice to her two children. As they were talking, Shelia's friend Natalie realized that the little chubby man in question is an international interpreter and an Ambassador to Spain, working in the Washington, D.C. office where Natalie works as an office assistant.

"He might be little in stature, but he is a *giant* in his career," Natalie declared. "*Girl,* if I were you, I'd let Little Joe go work for this man anytime. You just never know what kind of goldmine you might be facing! The *least* that could happen is that with the little money that Joey would make for himself, it would be a help to you," Natalie continues to say.

"I guess you are right," Shelia replied. "What harm could it do?"

Joey's three brothers were sitting on the couch watching cartoons, but also were listening to their mother's conversation. They all agreed about the decision to let Joey go work for this rich man.

"Who knows mama, it might take some of the worries off your shoulders," replied Thomas.

But after their mother and her friend had left the room, Claude said to Michael and Junior, "It will be one way to get rid of the little punk. I hope she lets him go *live* with the man."

Little did they all know, allowing Joey to work for this man was a bid to sell him into slavery. This sacrifice of Joey's time for a few dollars was not a good idea. You see; slavery comes in many different forms. It took four hundred years for African-Americans to be set free from the bonds of slavery. The kind of slavery that Joey was about to be subjected to would, after many years of struggle, take a miracle from God to set him free. But the miracle did not come until the scars of slavery had been deeply embedded. A look into the future of this innocent boy as an adult reveals him as a young man leading others to the saving grace of God through Jesus Christ. Not to mention that his brothers who despised him so and were so ashamed to own him as their little brother, would one day have to be fed and clothed by Joey. As compassionate as he could be, Joey would always avail himself whenever the phone would ring and either one of them would call for help. All but two of Joey's siblings ended up being seriously addicted to drugs or alcohol. But Joey was always there to help whenever called on.

Chapter 3

"The Suffering Slave"

Only one month has gone by and now this little black kid has gone from living in the ghetto, sharing a regular size bed with two of his brothers, to sharing a king size bed with satin sheets…with a little chubby guy named Bob. Yep, you heard it right. Bob was white and wealthy, but was also a very discrete pedophile whose love for little black boys transcended the norm. Joey was indeed an eye-catcher for those with like affections. He was quite tall for his age of thirteen; olive complexion, with unusually long eyelashes that fluttered each time he blinked his bedroom eyes. By now Joey had become used to what was now a life of comfort. Anything that his little heart desired, Bob would go out and buy it. Joey now had gone from wearing the dingy hand-me-downs, to the top-of-the-line brand name clothes. He had toys that he never dreamed of having and he was fed food that was fit for a king. Once a month, Bob would write a check for one hundred dollars and give it to Joey to give to his mother as a token of his appreciation for allowing Joey to come and live with him. Joey would pack his little overnight bag and go back home for an overnight stay with his family where everyone would sit around and listen to Joey talk about the lavish life that he was now living. They all would marvel at the stories as Joey talked about going to the theatres and traveling to New England to meet Bob's family. The stories, at times, made his brothers envy him. They would agree that Joey was *so* lucky to be where he was. Little did they know, the pain and inner struggles that Joey was suffering: trying to face himself every morning as he looked in the mirror.

Thinking about the activities that took place each night in bed with Bob was not easy for him to face. Although he knew in his heart that this was wrong, the thing that was so troubling to him was trying to figure why his mother did not see this as wrong. At times he even wondered if she knew at all what this man was really about. But then, the gifts, the money, the comfort of living a rich life somehow made the nightmares easy to bear. After about three years Bob's urges and desires for other young boys became the norm. Often, he would enlist Joey's help in luring other little boys in the neighborhood to his lair. Of course, money was the root behind this evil. And the little boys from the ghetto saw this as a great opportunity to make some money.

But Bob's little playhouse was about to be broken up. For it was an encounter with two brothers, who were classmates of Joey's that brought this little kingdom down. Eleven-year-old Jimmy and his thirteen-year-old brother Stewart were being raised by their father in the same housing complex where Joey and his family lived. One day, as Bob and Joey were grocery shopping at the same supermarket where Joey and his sister met Bob, Joey ran into Jimmy and Stewart. The three of them stood talking while Bob finished shopping. As Bob was entering the checkout line, he noticed these two handsome boys talking with Joey. As soon as they had loaded the groceries into the car, Bob began inquiring about the boys.

"So Joey, who were the two kids you were talking to?" Bob asked.

"Oh, just a couple of friends from the neighborhood," Joey replied.

"Well Joey you know, any friend of yours is a friend of mine."

As they drove home, they passed the two brothers as they were walking home. Bob blew his horn, Joey waved, and the two kids waved back.

The following morning as Bob was preparing for work and Joey for school, Bob gently began to talk about the two brothers, Stewart and Jimmy.

"So how well do you know them?" Bob asked.

Joey replied, "We all used to play together when I was living at home."

"So you guys are close friends, huh?"

"Well…sort of," Joey remarked.

"Listen, Joey, why not invite your two friends over tonight for some fun?"

"What…kind…of fun?" Joey asked nervously.

"Well you know, the usual," Bob said. "We'll have some popcorn, watch a movie and play a few games…"

"I don't know," Joey replied. "I don't think that would be a good idea. Their father is very strict, and usually don't allow them to go too far out of his sight."

"Well, just call them and see."

Joey walks over to the phone and nervously dials the number.

"Hello," came the voice on the other end.

"Mr. Fletcher, hi this is Joey Denison."

"Oh hi Joe, how are you doing?"

"Just fine. Is Jim or Stew around?"

"Yep, what's up?"

"Well Mr. Fletcher, I was just calling to see if they would like to come over to my house this evening to hang out and play a few games…that is if it's alright with you."

"Well Joe, I don't know. I am not going to be around tonight because I have to work real late. I have already made arrangements for the boys' aunt to pick them up and keep them for me until I get off from work."

"Well, Mr. Fletcher, they can stay over to my house until you get off from work. That way, you won't have to go across town to pick them up. You know, you have to pass my house to get to your job."

"I don't know, Joe. By the way, I hear you are not living at home with your mom anymore. Who is this you're living with?"

"His name is Bob McMillan, a friend of my mom's. He sort of adopted me for a while…you know, to give my mom a little help."

"Is he going to be alright with this?" Mr. Fletcher asked.

"Oh *sure*. He's a cool dude. He doesn't mind me having friends over."

"Well Joe, I still don't know about this…Tell you what, let me speak to this Mr. Bob."

"Okay, hold on." Joey covered the phone with his hand and yelled to Bob up stairs. "Pick up the phone!"

"Who is it?" came the response.

"It's Mr. Fletcher, the boys' dad. He just wants to talk to you to see if it's alright with you if Jimmy and Stewart come over."

Bob, nervously picked up the phone, cleared his throat and began talking. "This is Bob McMillan."

"Yeah, hello, this is James Fletcher, Jimmy and Stewart's father. Joey has called asking for my boys to come over to your house this evening and hang out with him. There are a few things that I would like know before I give permission for my boys to come over there."

"What things would you like to know?" Bob asked nervously.

"Well… basic parent questions. For starters, is it all right with you should I allow my boys to come over with Joey after school? And secondly, will they be safe?"

"Well Mr. Fletcher, as I told Joey, any friend of his is a friend of mine. Certainly if Joey wants your boys to come over tonight, it will be just fine with me. They won't be in my way at *all*."

"One more thing Mr. McMillan…"

"…Please call me Bob."

"Okay, Bob, what kind of games will they be playing?"

"Joey has some video games that he enjoys playing. They probably will watch one of Joey's movies, eat popcorn and junk food and talk school stuff. You know how kids are now days."

"There is also one other thing."

"What is it, Mr. Fletcher?" Bob asked.

"I know today is Friday. Tomorrow the boys don't have to get up for school, but I have to work late tonight. Will there be a problem if the boys stay there until around eleven tonight until I get off from work? I will definitely pick them up on my way home."

"Oh sure!" Bob replied with much excitement in his voice. "They will be alright. You can pick them up whenever you can."

"Well, tell Joe for me that I will drop the boys off around six tonight."

"Alright, thanks. You have a good day."

"You too."

Bob got dressed and went downstairs with a big smile on his face. Joey looked up from his bowl of cereal, and asked the question, "So what did he say?"

"Everything is set for this evening. The boys will be dropped off around six. Just relax, Joey," Bob continues. "Everything is going to be alright."

"I don't know. I just hope you don't try anything with these two."

"Anything like what?"

"You know what I mean. You don't know how protective Mr. Fletcher is about his kids. I…just don't want to be in the middle of any trouble."

"Get your book bag, here's your money. It's time for the bus and time for me to get to work. Listen Joey; don't mess up your day in school worrying about nothing. This evening is your time to enjoy your friends."

"Okay. See you later."

While standing on the curb waiting for the school bus to come, Joey started getting butterflies in his stomach as he thought about the consequences that could occur if things went wrong tonight. As much as Bob tried to assure him that all be go well, somehow, Joey knew trouble was just around the corner. To Bob, it really did not matter. For he was so overconfident with himself, he just knew nothing could ever go wrong. After all, he was discrete. He was in charge of every thing. This was his house.

Nothing could go wrong as long as he was in control of things. What Bob did not know, was that he was not in control. It was only a matter of time when *He who is really in charge* would allow Bob's little kingdom to be torn down. As it is written in the Holy Bible, (Galatians 6:7); *"Be not deceived, God is not mocked: For whatsoever a man soweth, that shall he also reap."* This night is the night that the reaping days for Mr. Bob would commence.

Chapter 4

"The Last Night in Captivity"

The clock over the mantle in the living room was about to strike six. Just then, the doorbell rang. Bob came out of the kitchen. Joey came up the stairs from his game room; the unused portion of the basement that Bob had remolded into a cozy little rec room with all of the trappings for any visiting kid from the neighborhood. Bob opened the door to find two bright-eyed youngsters accompanied by a tall slender man with a big smile on his face.

"Good evening," the voice came from the other side of the storm door.

"Good evening. You must be Mr. Fletcher. And *these* two broncos must be Jim and Stew. I'm Bob McMillan, Joey's guardian. Come on in." They all came in.

"Hey Joey!" Stew said.

Joey smiled and with a burst of excitement asked, "Are you two ready for some fun in the game room?"

"Joey, why don't you take the fellows on down and I'll be down shortly to see what snacks you guys may want."

"Alright, let's go!"

As the boys left the living room Mr. Fletcher spoke, "Are you sure having the boys over is not an inconvenience?"

"Of course not. I'm delighted to have them in my home. They are going to have so much fun."

"Well, I really appreciate it," replied Mr. Fletcher. "I've got to get to work. I'll drop back by to pick up the boys as soon as the shift ends. That should be around eleven thirty."

"Alright," Bob said. "Drive careful and we will see you later."

Bob watched James Fletcher pull off and then closed the door with a sigh of relief. Bob went up stairs to his room to finish some paper work from his job and to mentally prepare himself for the challenging evening that lied ahead. His heart was pounding with excitement.

Meanwhile, Joey is having the time of his life entertaining his two best friends from his old neighborhood. They, of course, are in a kid's heaven. They are overwhelmed at all of the toys, games and neat stuff that Joey has to play with. As the boys get settled in playing a serious game of Nintendo, Stewart began asking questions about Joey and his relationship with Bob. "Joey man, how did you get to be so lucky? To live with somebody who can give you all this stuff? And by the way, why does he give you all this stuff? Does he do anything else with his money other than buy you stuff…"

"Never mind that," Jimmy blurted out, "What I want to know is if he is looking for another kid to adopt. Man, I sure would give it a try."

By now Joey is uncomfortable with all of the questions, so he smiled his way through the inquiry. Joey finally responded by saying, "Bob is a good man who never had kids of his own. So he gets a thrill out of treating me like I'm his kid. He is just a nice little chubby dude."

"Yeah, a real Humpty Dumpty," replied Stew.

They all burst into laughter behind Stewart's humor.

About 8:30, they suddenly hear footsteps in the stairway. They looked around and it is Bob with a great big grin on his face. "Are you fellows having fun? It looks like a real video den down here. Who is winning?"

Joey was the first one to nervously speak up and say, "Sure, we're doing just fine, Bob."

"Well, I am glad to hear that you are having fun, Joe. But what about Stew and Jim? Are you guys having fun?"

"Oh yes sir!" they both answered in unison.

"We are really enjoying ourselves," said Jimmy.

"Now *that's* what I want to hear!" Bob said. "Well, when you guys get tired of playing down here, we have another playroom upstairs…don't we Joey?"

19

Joey looked up at Bob intensely and replies, "We're doing just fine down here."

But as excited as he was to be having so much fun downstairs, Jimmy could not imagine being introduced to another room filled with all of the entertaining things that he had only dreamed about. So he excitedly responded, "Come on Joey! Take us up to the other game room. We can always come back down here."

"Well, I'm going to go on up and pop some more popcorn and I will also open another bag of chips for you guys when you come up. Joey, why don't you grab some of those fudgesicles in the fridge on your way up?"

Joey looked up at Bob as he is mounting the stairway and replies, "Bob if it's alright with you we will stay down here for a little while longer."

Bob cunningly looked around at Joey and said, "Is that what your guests want to do?"

Not realizing what kind of games they would be playing, the brothers both spoke up and said, "It's alright with us Joe. We would love to go to the other playroom."

Joey dropped his head like a kid who has just lost his best friend and responded by saying, "If you're sure you want to go upstairs, then we will go."

And so it was settled, to the upstairs game room they headed.

Now the game room upstairs was a huge and spacious room with a big screen television, card table, and a book case loaded with some of Bob's favorite videos that he would later have to explain as being some of his "teaching videos". And of course, there was a large air mattress with several fluffy throw pillows on it.

As the boys entered the room, Bob stood up from his beanbag chair and welcomed the boys in. Poor Joey was so nervous that he could hardly think straight.

"So boys, why don't we start by watching a movie? Have a seat. Get comfortable if you like."

The boys followed Joey over to the air mattress and they all sat down, pulled their shoes off and tried to get as comfortable as they could.

"I just thought it would be a good idea to get away from the video games for a while and relax and enjoy a movie or two."

"So what are we watching?" Jim asked.

Joey spoke up, "Bob, why don't we watch that new Matrix movie that you bought the other day for me?"

"Well Joey, let's see what our guests might be interested in watching. Boys, you have a choice...the Matrix flick or one of my teaching videos that I made."

"What exactly is your video about?" Jimmy asked.

"Well, you see, the movie is about a scout leader and his troops that did a lot of camping that involved roughing it in the wild. And not knowing much about scouting, sometimes surviving with only a pocket knife and book of matches for fire..."

"I've seen that one many times," Joey interrupted. "I think y'all would like the Matrix movie better."

Bob looked over at Joey with disgust and said to him in a rebuking kind of way, "Joey, let the boys decide for *themselves*."

Stewart spoke and said, "It really don't matter. Our dad took us to see the Matrix flick when it first came out. It's a good movie; I don't mind seeing it again or we can watch Mr. Bob's video."

"Joey, I'll tell you what," said Bob, "Since you've seen the scout video enough, give the fellows here the chance to see it and maybe you can go down to the kitchen and pop some more popcorn. I forgot to do it on my way up from the basement. Besides, the video is only 30 minutes long."

"What kind of movie lasts only 30 minutes?" Stew asked.

"Well it's sort of like a documentary...only with fun stuff in it," Bob replied. "Just sit back, relax and you'll see."

Joey backed out of the room looking back at Bob as he dropped down on the air mattress with his two friends who are unaware of the game that they are about to play. The "teaching video" is a 30-minute dip into the awful world of child

21

pornography. The video starts off with a chubby little man and two young boys supposedly camping out and surviving in the wilderness. As they settle in their tent, the scoutmaster politely asks the two boys to undress and get comfortable for the evening. Because the two kids in the video were two paid child porn stars, they obliged their scoutmaster and the rest is history. At this point, Bob was now ready to make a move on his two little scouts. Jimmy and his brother Stewart were both sitting in the dark gazing at this video that had them feeling scared and somewhat curious about the things that were taking place.

Quietly, Jimmy looked over at Stew and whispered, "What kind of movie is this?"

Bob spoke up and made the suggestion, "Why don't we take off our clothes and get more comfortable?"

"Should we be doing something like this?" Jim asked.

"Oh sure," Bob said. "It's alright to have a little fun. It's alright to explore new things."

Half convinced that Bob's way of having fun was okay, the two boys nervously slipped out of their clothes and Bob gave them a blanket to cover themselves. The rest of the evening's events in the upstairs game room were history, which ended with Bob going into his wallet and pulling out two crisp fifty dollar bills and giving them to the boys as a token of gratitude for being so submissive to him.

Joey, on the other hand, spent the last hour and a half sitting in his room silently crying and trying to block out the familiar noises coming from the game room across the hall. Suddenly, the game room door opened, Joey quickly wiped his face and went to the door. He stood and watched as his two best friends shuffled their way out of the room with their heads hanging down in shame. So to compensate for such an embarrassing moment, Joey begins laughing and joking about the video.

"What a silly game those two kids were playing! Huh, guys?"

Jimmy looked up at Joey and said, "Unlike the two kids in the video, we got paid for playing the game."

Before anything else could be said, there came a knock at the door downstairs. Bob came out of the room smiling like a Cheshire cat and said, "Well boys, that must be your dad at the door. I hope you had a lot of fun. And remember…nobody has to know about the secret fun that we had."

The boys looked up at him and said quietly, "Yeah, thanks for everything."

"Joey," Bob said, "walk the fellows to the door and give my regards to Mr. Fletcher. I am turning in for the night."

Joey went ahead of them down the stairs, opened the door, and let Mr. Fletcher in."

"Are the boys ready to go, Joe?" Mr. Fletcher asked.

"Hey dad," Jim said.

"Wow, you boys really look worn out. What did Joey have y'all doing, rock climbing? Listen Joey, thanks for everything. Tell your dad…I mean Mr. McMillan, thanks for me."

"No problem," Joey said. "He's in bed by now. And he said to give his regards."

"Well we're off. Have a good night, Joey."

"See 'ya, Stew. See 'ya, Jim. I'll call you guys tomorrow sometime." Joey stood in the doorway and watched as they pulled off. As he turned around to close and lock the door, he was startled to see Bob coming down the steps.

"I thought you were in bed," Joey said.

"Well I am on my way to bed. Just wanted a drink of water before turning in…I had a *lot* of fun," Bob said chuckling.

On his way up the stairs to his room, Joey looked down at Bob and said, "I just hope this does not come up again."

From time to time, Joey would fall by his bedside and pray before going to sleep, especially whenever he was troubled. This was one of those nights that Joey prayed to his Father and asked for protection and peace in his heart. Joey's Father in heaven knew the struggles that he faced. And because of His love for him, He was soon to bring an end to such misery. Joey had no idea that the events of this evening would bring an end to his captivity. Often, Joey felt as though he was to blame for the struggles that he had to face from time to time living in the secret world of pedophilia.

After all, he was only a confused teenager whose life was spent being raised in a dysfunctional family; with brothers who despised him for his dreams of one day becoming somebody great and a mother who was only interested in ways to earn extra money as long as it did not lead her anywhere she did not want to go. Shelia took up with a man named Curtis that she met at a neighborhood dance. At that time, her youngest child was only two and her oldest, Lela, was only fourteen. Lela was the only one who remembered what their real dad looked like before he walked off and left them one cold night. So Curtis was the only dad that most of them could relate to.

Curtis was a street man who never kept a public job. He made all of his money hustling the streets. He was a drug user and quite abusive to Shelia and the kids. So even if Shelia saw an opportunity for a better life outside of the Salley Whitlock Housing Projects, she wouldn't take it for fear of what Curtis would do to her. Joey was the one whom Curtis picked on the most, so there was never much love between the two of them. The events that took place after Bob's rendezvous with the Fletcher boys only intensified the feelings of dislike between the two of them. As a matter of fact, even Joey's brothers took advantage of the opportunity to accuse Joey of willing luring the boys into the Bob's lair.

Chapter 5

"The Fall of Humpty Dumpty"

By the time James Fletcher had arrived back home from a tiring night of work, the boys had fallen asleep in the car. It was sort of a struggle trying to get both boys awake, out of the car and into the apartment.

"You boys don't have to worry about taking a shower before bed since it's so late," Mr. Fletcher said. By this time, the boys were wide awake and remembering the events of the evening. So Jim spoke up and said,

"It's not too late for me dad. I feel that a shower will do me some good."

"Me too," said Stewart.

"Well you don't have too, it is really late and tomorrow is Saturday."

"We still want to take a shower, dad, before going to bed."

"Well, alright. Just throw your clothes into the hallway and I'll put them with the other clothes for laundry tomorrow."

The boys, one by one, took turns undressing. Jim went first into the shower and when he had finished, he waited for Stew to finish before he climbed into bed. While lying in bed, both boys were restless and could not fall asleep. So they began whispering about what had happened.

Stewart said to Jimmy, "How do you feel about what happened tonight? Do you think it was right?"

Jimmy replied, "Nah, I don't think it was right. And I hope dad doesn't ever find out. Man he would *kill* us if he knew!"

"You're right," Stewart said. "It happened, it's over, and that's that. I promise you dad will never hear from me. I'm really tired. Let's just try to get some sleep. Tomorrow is new day, and all of this will be behind us. Good night, Jim."

The next morning while the boys were sleeping in, Mr. Fletcher decided to do the laundry before he woke the boys for

25

breakfast. As he was sorting the clothes, he came across the boys' jeans that they had on the night before. He attempted to empty the pockets to make sure nothing was left in them that would stain the rest of the laundry. Once while doing laundry, an ink pen was left and it stained the other articles in that particular load. Ever since then "Mr. Mom" makes a thorough search of all pants pockets before tossing them into the laundry.

"What is this?" he said as he was searching Stewart's pants.

To his surprise, it was a crisp, new fifty-dollar bill. Jim's jeans were the next item in the pile of laundry to be searched. Once again, a crisp fifty-dollar bill was found. Mr. Fletcher stood there in front of the washer puzzled with mixed emotions trying to figure out where this money may have come from. He finally said to himself, "I hope these boys didn't steal this money while they were over at Joey's house last night…Oh God have mercy, it's the only explanation that I can come up with." With this thought in mind, he ran upstairs to the boys' bedroom. As he entered the door, he started calling out their names.

"James! Stewart! Wake up! Get up now!"

The boys were startled out of their sleep and began shouting back at their dad in fear, "What is it, dad. What's happened? Why are you screaming so loud?"

"I need to talk to you. I was downstairs about to do the wash. And as I was cleaning out your pants pockets when I ran across *this*."

Standing there in the middle of the floor was Mr. Fletcher holding the money that Bob had given them on last night.

"So *tell* me," Mr. Fletcher shouted, "where did all of this money come from? Did y'all steal this money out of Joey's house last night?"

The boys immediately sat up in their bunk beds. While wiping the sleep out of their eyes, Jimmy began speaking for the two of them.

"No, dad. We didn't steal any money from Joey's house!"

"Well, if you didn't steal it, did you perhaps find it on the floor and thought that maybe it was alright to keep it? Y'all got to

26

tell me the truth! What I *do* know is this money just didn't fall out of the sky. You boys know how much I wish I could give you money like this one day. But right now I can't. So I *know* this money did not come out of this house. So *where* did it come from?"

"Dad, the money was given to us as a present," explained Stewart.

Jimmy looks over at his brother with tears in his eyes and begins to apologetically explain the horror away. "You see dad, Mr. Bob gave us the money as a gift for doing some things for him last night. We're both sorry...we didn't know that we shouldn't have taken the money. We'll get dressed and walk over to Joey's house and give the money back to Mr. Bob...won't we, Stew?"

"Yeah dad, we'll take it all back. I guess it was a lot of money to take."

"Wait a minute, Jimmy. Did you say the money is a gift?"

"Yeah, Dad."

"Something is still strange about all of this. What on *earth* did y'all help him do to earn so much money? That's what I want to know."

Silence filled the room as the boys tried mentally to connect with each other for an appropriate answer.

"Alright, since neither one of you wants to tell me the truth, I will call Mr. Bob myself."

As he turned to go out of the room to place the call, Stewart burst out in tears, immediately followed by Jimmy. "Dad, we are sorry, we didn't know. We...thought it was okay. We're *really* sorry. We won't do it again. It was *our* fault; you don't have to call Mr. Bob. He didn't force us to do anything against our will."

James Fletcher stood frozen in the hallway as he listened to the cries of agony coming from behind him. "Wait a minute! Hold up. What are you saying? Why are you boys all of a sudden so upset? Never mind, what I need to know is what exactly *did you do* for Bob to give you this money?"

Pulling himself together as much as he could, Stewart began to describe the events of the past evening. "Dad we really

had a good time playing with Joey in his game room downstairs.
Then Mr. Bob came down and asked us to come upstairs and hang
out in the game room up there. At first, Joey tried to convince him
that we were all having enough fun where we were. But Mr. Bob
was sort of forceful and so he convinced us to come upstairs to
play. But, dad, we didn't know what kind of games he wanted us to
play…did we, Jim?"

"No, dad, we didn't."

"As a matter of fact, we thought there would be more video
games and stuff like that. So he invited us into this big game room
that had a large mattress with pillows all over it. Then there was
also a big TV and a bookcase that was full of movies…"

"*Oh…my God,*" James Fletcher said as he began to realize
what had really happened to his boys. "Before you go on any
further, am I to assume that Mr. Bob put in a movie, invited y'all
to watch and then…did…those…things with y'all that were in the
movie?"

The boys, too embarrassed to say anything, simply dropped
their heads as if to say yes. As they sat up in their bunk beds,
watching their father fall to his knees and sob with so much agony
that it made them weep even more. But after he got control of
himself, he called the boys to him, embraced them with love and
assured them that they were not to feel guilty or feel as if they were
to blame. He rose from his knees, wiped his eyes, cleared his throat
and remarked, "Poor Joey. If that kid remains in that house any
longer, he will be damaged for life. I have got to find a way to put
an end to this madness. I <u>must</u> bring this Humpty Dumpty down--
You boys go back to bed and try to put this nightmare behind you.
I will take care of this. Don't y'all worry, just rest."

As they climbed back into bed, they watched their father
exit the room and close the door behind him. The morning for
them had been so stressful it did not take much for them to fall
back to sleep. James Fletcher sat in the kitchen looking out of the
window at the people scurrying about with their usual Saturday
morning activities. He said to himself, "I wonder who else might
be a victim of this man's evil deeds." With that question and others

28

running through his mind, he reached up from where he was sitting for the telephone hanging on the wall and began dialing Bob McMillan's number. Not really knowing exactly what he was going to say to this man, he braced himself as he waited.

"Hello," came the voice on the other end.

"Hello, Mr. McMillan?"

"Yes, this is he."

"This is James Fletcher."

Immediately there was a silence from the other end of the phone line.

"Oh, Mr. Fletcher…what a surprise to hear from you so early this morning! How are the boys doing? Still sleeping, I'm sure."

"Listen Bob, let's get straight to the point," replied James. "All I want you to do is hear me out, so do not *speak* unless I ask you to."

Bob's heart was about to jump out of his chest. At this point, he was so nervous he had to sit down. "All right, Mr. Fletcher," he replied.

James continued by saying, "I know what you did last night to my boys. I found the money that you gave them for allowing you to do what you did to them last night. First of all, let me start off by saying I think it is a scandal and shame that you have to use little boys for your sexual fantasies. I don't understand it, nor do I care to understand. But *here* is what you are going to do--Because you used my boys I have no doubt that you are using little Joey as well for your fantasies. Here is what you will do--today! Somehow, you are going to find a way and a reason to tell Joey that you are going to take him back home today…"

"Oh no!" replied Bob. "He is going to be devastated. I can't just uproot him like that! He is so happy living here with me…"

"You listen to me, you pervert!" shouts James. "I don't care *how* you do it, but by the end of the day, you are going to take that boy back home. The next thing you are going to do is start making preparations to *leave this city*. I don't care *where* you go. You *have* to leave this city."

29

"And if I <u>don't</u>, what can you do about it?" Bob said.

"Listen you little fat pervert, you've got until six this evening to take that boy back home! If you don't, my boys and me are going to the police and file a report against you. Also, you have thirty days to get out of town. If you have not moved in thirty days, I will do all in my power to have you locked up for *life*. Do you hear me?"

buzzz… The telephone connection was now dead. Bob had slammed the phone down in anger, leaving Mr. Fletcher hanging on the other end. As he hung up the phone, the clock struck nine a.m. James Fletcher began a countdown for Bob. "Nine hours to go and this nightmare will be over for Joey and the boys."

What Mr. Fletcher did not know was this was just the beginning of a rough journey for Joey that would one day position him to help others who had been subjected to such depravity. You see at this point, all of Joey's days had not come in.

Chapter 6

"The Sixth Hour"

It was twelve noon. Three of the nine hours given to Bob to release Joey had past. Joey always slept late on Saturday mornings until about noon. However this particular Saturday morning, Joey was awakened by a sobbing Bob standing over his bed pleading for him to get up.

"I am getting up. Why are you crying?" Joey asked Bob.

"Joey I'm *so* sorry," Bob replied. "I am going to have to take you back home--If only I had listened to you. I would not be in this mess."

"Why...tell me...what in the world is going on?" Joey asked as he leapt out of bed.

"Well, I received a phone call from Mr. Fletcher this morning. Somehow, he has found out about last night and the events that took place in the game room. So he called me and informed me that if I didn't take you back to your mother's house by six o'clock tonight...he would report me to the police."

Joey began to scream hysterically, "No...no, he can't do this, can he Bob? Even if the boys did talk it would be your word against theirs, wouldn't it? You *see* Bob," Joey added, "I *told* you it was a bad idea. Now *your* greed has cost me my home!"

"Joey, I am *so* sorry. There is really not much that I can do. I *have* to take you back home. Not only that, Fletcher also gave me thirty days to leave the city. And if I don't, he promises to still go to the police...this man means business.

"Isn't that blackmail or something like that?" Joey asked.

"Well it really doesn't matter, Joe. You see, I am under suspicion with the police department involving charges brought against me by another kid and his parents. If I am charged again, they will definitely throw the book at me--My hands are tied, I have to do it or else. So please Joey, I will help you pack as much stuff as we can get in the trunk and back seat of the car."

31

The thought of going back to the ghetto for this little rejected kid was a bit overwhelming. As Joey began to weep, the two of them stood in the middle of the room embracing and weeping together. The remainder of the day was spent packing Joey's things: his name brand clothes, shoes and every Nintendo game that Bob has bought for him. Because Joey wanted to take his mahogany bedroom set, Bob went around the corner and rented a cargo van. Joey went home with more stuff than there was enough room for. Before they left, Bob made Joey his favorite lunch: oodles of noodles with a spam, lettuce and tomato sandwich. After lunch, Joey called his mother and told her that he was on his way home. It took her a while to believe him, but she finally said to him, "Come on home, baby, if you want to."

Joey did not go into detail about the reasons behind him returning home. He just said, "Bob has to move out of the state soon." And so after about another half hour of lingering around in what he had come to know as his home, Joey finally looked over at Bob and said, "I'm ready now."

As they drove down the boulevard in the direction of Whitlock projects, there was an eerie silence hovering in the van. Joey's family lived in one of the corner units, so as they began to approach the front of the house, Bob said to Joey, "I believe I'll park around the side, so that we will have access to either the front or side door." Joey did not comment.

After Bob stopped the van, Joey immediately got out of the van and proceeded to walk toward the door. Shelia, Joey's mom, was standing in the door watching as he came up the walk. As the two of them made eye contact, Shelia flung the door open and ran out to meet him. As they embraced, Joey held back the tears and even tried to smile. Shelia, seeing the struggle in his face, simply said to him, "It's going to be alright baby. You gon' be fine. Go on in the house and get your brothers to come out and help you with your stuff."

Joey's brothers and two of his sisters had already made it to the front door. They all came out in silence and began to unload the van. While the van was being unloaded, Shelia walked over to

Bob and began inquiring about the sudden move. "So what is this that I hear 'bout you leaving town?" she asked.

"Well, Shelia, it's all sort of complicated. My company's New England office is going through a major downsizing, so my boss wants me to go up and help keep things in order. I really didn't have much of a choice. It was either go to New England or stay and risk the chance of losing my job."

Shelia looked directly into Bob's eyes and said to him, "Are you *sure* that's the reason?"

Bob nervously replied, "Oh, I'm sure….what other reason could there be?"

"I don't really know," Shelia replied. "Joey seems to be a bit shaken behind this."

"Well, yes he is. Joey had become very comfortable in my house. And of course, I tried to give him a life that he could appreciate and cherish even after he is grown."

"Well, it looks like they're about finished unloading the van--I have to tend to my baby and make sure his brothers don't mess with any of his nice things. Thanks for helping Joey."

"Tell Joey…I'll call him just before I move." Bob turned to get back in the van. Standing across the street staring in his direction was Mr. Fletcher with his two sons. Bob slowly got back in the van and James Fletcher never took his eyes off of him. As Bob pulled out into the street, James Fletcher continued to watch him until he could no longer see the van in the distance. Turning to go back inside, he called to his boys and said,

"The nightmare is over. I think we all can sleep a little better now that Joey is in a safer place. I hope this mess has not done too much damage to him."

Bob is likened to the foolish builder. As mentioned in St. Matthew 7:26-27,

> *"And every one that heareth these saying of mine, doeth them not, shall be likened unto a foolish man which built his house upon the sand. (27) And the rain descended, and the floods came, and the winds*

blew, and beat upon that house, and it fell: and
great was the fall of it."

Bob never regained his seat of wickedness in high places.
For the next ten to twenty years, his life spiraled downward from
health problems to a failing career.

Chapter 7

"The Family-The Familiar"

Three weeks had now come and gone. Joey was settled in with his mom and siblings. At first, they all treated him as if he was a king's kid. (He was *indeed* the King's kid.) Joey came home dressed differently, talking as if he had been raised in royalty all of his life. He had things to play with that no other kid in the neighborhood had. And as handsome as he was before he left, he looked even *more* handsome with his new wardrobe.

Impressed as they may have been, envy and jealousy eventually took a seat at the head of the family table. An even greater streak of jealousy began to surface between Joey and mostly his brothers. They all envied him for the new stuff, the new clothes and the new and different style of living that he brought into the house. Soon the fights began and Joey was back to looking for love in all the wrong places.

While living with Bob, Joey had met some of Bob's "finer" colleagues. One in particular was a couple from Sweden who were members in the same professional organization as Bob. They were a husband and wife team of linguists; over in the U.S. on a grant studying the difference between the dialects of African-Americans based on geographical locations. Joey had been in their presence on several occasions and they were quite impressed with him. They were a couple that had no children, and had once approached Bob about the possibility of adopting Joey. Of course at that particular time, Bob was not interested in giving Joey up to *any* one.

However, about three months after he had returned home, he received a phone call from this couple. They spoke kindly with his mother for a while and then they asked to speak to Joey. To Joey's surprise and much to his delight, they were calling to see if he would be interested in living with them. This would be on a trial basis, for the purpose of studying his family's dialect as a model for an inner-city speech development project. Their interest was mainly focused on a dialect only used in the lower-class African-American neighborhoods known as Ebonics.

This was an offer that neither Joey, nor his mother, could refuse. For Joey, it meant having another shot at the good life. And for Shelia, it meant another monthly check for her to help support the rest of the family. And so it happened. A meeting was set with Shelia, Joey, an attorney and the Hofflingers. Negotiations were made and agreed upon by both parties. Shelia was to receive a stipend each month along with an updated report of the progress of the study that was being performed. Also at this meeting, Joey learned that Bob had indeed resigned from his position and moved northeast just like he said to take a different position as a speech therapist. It did not phase Joey one bit. His focus was on getting another chance to live the good life that to him was only outside of the Salley Whitlock Housing Projects.

Off to the posh suburbs of Richmond, Virginia, Joey went. As they crossed the Potomac River--leaving the city limits of D.C., Joey looked back and thought to himself,

"When I come back to *this* place again, I will have made it in life."

What Joey did not know was his stay in Richmond would be short lived and rejection he was soon again to experience. Nevertheless, Joey went to Richmond and enjoyed a couple of months of living a good life with the Hofflinger family. While in Richmond, Joey attended private school. He was a member of the soccer team. He was taken to the theatre regularly and he wore the best clothes that money could buy. He was fed from a king's table. He enjoyed and became quite fond of Swedish cuisine. At the age of sixteen, he was living in the lap of luxury…until the day the Hofflingers decided to split up and go their separate ways.

Being as young as he was, it was hard for him to understand what could have possibly happened to cause this family to separate. He asked questions that he thought would give him clarity, but it was never reached. The only thing that Mrs.

Hofflinger, (Latish as he called her) would say to him was, "I'm tired of being number two."

And so it was, two weeks later, Latish came into Joey's room, sat on his bed, and explained to him that he would have to go back to live with his family. After months of being away from the much-dreaded Salley Whitlock Housing Projects, Joey was facing the reality of going back...*again.* The agony, at times, was a bit overwhelming for Joey. Not only was he about to leave the best private school in the state, he was also leaving his friends that he had become so attached to behind.

One very special friend was Nunzio, an Italian kid whose parents had immigrated to the U.S. when he was about six years old. His father's first job in the U.S. was a baker for a local pastry shop, but now ten years later, he was the owner of a chain of bakeries. Joey and Nunzio both played soccer on the same team. They had become so close that at times, the other boys on the team would tease them about their relationship. Joey had accepted leaving Richmond, but he could not stand the thought of having to be separated from the *only* person in his life that he was able to connect with. But as luck may have it, Joey had to build himself another bridge, get over it and leave Nunzio behind. Back to the furnace of affliction Joey had to go.

And because all of his days had not come in, he had no idea that his heavenly Father was actually choosing him, molding him, purging him, maturing him and even anointing him for the next great level in his life. The sufferings of this young man named Joey were making him to be the perfect example of:

"The greater the suffering, the greater the anointing."

Chapter 8

"On the Road Again"

Joey was on the road again, crossing the river and going back to the ghetto; feeling rejected and hurt once more. It was a hot Saturday August morning that Latish drove Joey back to D.C. to be with his family. She had talked with Joey's mother earlier in the week about returning him. Shelia, of course, understood the difficulties behind a broken marriage. So she was quite sympathetic with Latish, even though the monthly check would stop coming. So when they arrived, Shelia was sitting on the stoop waiting to receive her prodigal child back home.

Joey's return home was not as bad as he thought it would have been. For one thing, his two oldest brothers were now eighteen and twenty, so they had moved out on their own. It only left Junior Curtis, his youngest brother to contend with. And even Junior was not a problem to get along with now that the other two were gone. Joey had his own bedroom and bed to sleep in, so it was not as bad as he had imagined it. The only person he had to contend with was Big Curtis, the man whom his mother had taken up with…whom everybody else called 'dad'.

But Joey knew that Big Curtis was not his father. And for some odd reason Big Curtis did not like Joey much. In the past, he never talked much to Joey as he did to the other boys. And when he did, it was always with a harsh voice. So Joey stayed away from him as much as possible.

Shelia took Joey down to Carver, the local high school, to start the process of transferring his school records from Richmond. Two weeks later, they received a notice from the school guidance counselor with Joey's class assignments. Joey, going on seventeen, an up and rising junior, was a sight to behold. He was tall, slender, with a perfect complexion, and teeth as white as snow. Every girl at Carver High wanted to date Joey. Joey became an overnight success with popularity. Most of the kids who attended Carver lived in the same projects that Joey lived in. They all knew of Joey from middle school, but had not seen him for a couple of years. So everybody was impressed with the Joey who has now evolved from his childhood cocoon to a teenager of distinction. At that time, it was still a mystery whether or not Joey was seriously affected, sexually, mentally, or socially by the years spent living with the neighborhood pedophile. The few people who actually knew about the horror that went on could only hope in time that Joey would be able to share his experience to help other misguided families; that they should be more cautious of dangerous neighborhood predators like Mr. Bob.

Chapter 9

"The Days are Coming In"

With only two more years to be completed in high school, Joey was excited about pursuing a career as a journalist or teacher of journalism. Having met with the high school guidance counselor, Joey applied for entrance into several universities. Unfortunately for him, his life is about to take another detour to his destiny when out of nowhere he is followed by and constantly harassed by one Carver High's bullies.

Joey was quite popular and well liked by all of his classmates except for this one guy whom every one knew as "Bullet Head". Bullet Head's real name was Tracey, but of course being the bully that he was, he did not take to anyone calling him by his real name. Every day, Bullet Head would wait for Joey to arrive at school. And as soon as he saw Joey, he would walk behind him, pluck Joey behind the head and call him names that would belittle his image with the girls in school. There were days that Joey would refuse to take the abuse, so on several occasions a heated argument would break out between the two. Both of them lived in the same housing project, so it seemed as if Bullet Head knew something about Joey that no one else knew. And as far as Joey was concerned, it was secret that he was determined to keep to himself.

As soon as the first bell rang, the two of them would retreat to their 1st period classes. But then at the end of the school day, Joey would have to face the bully head-on. Without a single person who was willing to stand in his defense, the only comfort Joey would get was while walking home from school each day, he would pass three churches. Though he never ventured to go inside of either church, *somehow* as he would pass by and look upon the beautiful stained glass windows, he would feel as sense of belonging.

The harassment lasted for so long until one morning, when Joey got up and got dressed for school. But instead of going to school, Joey went down to the recruiter's office and enlisted himself into the army. Two days later, he was shipped off to boot camp. There, he successfully completed six weeks of extensive training for the United States Army. From boot camp, Joey endured six more weeks of quarter master's training. After he was sent to Japan for a one-year tour of duty, his life took a serious turn from exposure to alcohol and drugs. From Japan, to Utah, to the Persian Gulf, he served his country and became deeper involved with the partying scene. As low as Joey had sunk into the bondage of alcohol, drugs and sexual promiscuity it was, however, not too low that his heavenly Father could not reach him and pull him up.

It was on his last assignment, stationed at Fort A.P. Hill, that he met a young lady whom God used to usher in the rest of his days. They met, fell in love and were married six months later by her uncle who was a retired army chaplain pastoring a little church not far from the base. The first two years of his marriage were spent being witnessed to by his wife, Diana and other members of the little congregation. By now, the effects of his childhood ordeals and the rejection that he suffered from his family had hardened Joey. So talking to him about a God of love and concern was something that he was not ready to hear. Diana was raised in the church, so being the wife of a non-Christian somehow boosted her to seek a deeper and closer walk with the Lord. In the meantime, Joey was discharged from the army and landed a job closer to the suburbs of his hometown. So in an area called Prince William, they settled and began raising a family.

Two boys were born to this union. So, in an attempt to be a good father to his children, Joey followed Diana to a revival service that was being held at the church where Diana was now a member. After that night, Joey realized what was missing in his life: a relationship with the Lord. So that night, as the invitation to discipleship was being extended, Joey was the first of seventeen converts who accepted Jesus as Lord and Savior. Joey's days are now rolling in like a flood. It was as if God was in a hurry to do a new thing in his life. In this little congregation, that feeling of belonging that he used to experience while walking home from school every day as he walked past those three churches, was now a reality.

Joey's relationship with God increased, but his relationship to Diana took a turn for the worst. Little by little, argument by argument, the relationship between Joey and his wife of ten years was stretched out of proportion. *It was the little foxes at the bottom of the grapevine that destroyed the whole vine.* The little "foxes" were the small arguments, disagreements and dislikes that were never resolved; in time driving a wedge between the two of them. Soon their affection for each other had turned into contempt for each other. They tried to stick it out for the sake of the kids, but it did not take long for even that to wear thin. One Saturday morning, a conversation about the past led Diana to ask Joey to leave.

"I am so sorry you can't explain the loss of interest in our romance Joey," Diana remarked.

"Well if you had been through the things that I have been through, you would too find it hard to talk about," Joey replied.

"Are you telling me, that even after going to counseling with the pastor, you are not willing to give it a second chance, Joey?"

"What I am *telling* you Diana is--Yes the counseling with Reverend Scott was good, but somehow I just don't feel that it has solved all of our problems. When *I* try to talk to you about what I feel is the root of our problems, your only response is 'you should have built a bridge and gotten over that mess by now.' I just don't see us moving on without dealing with our past issues."

"Alright! I have heard enough, Joe. I think it's about time we made the decision to go our separate ways. Because if you think I am going to sit around and listen to you *complain* about your past hurt and disappointments over the way your family treated you...*you* are terribly mistaken."

"So what are you saying, Diana?"

"I am saying, go pack your stuff and go! I am too tired to talking about this again. Just go! The boys will be all right. I know you will still be a good father to them, but right now I think it's time to bring this fight to an end."

The rest of that day Joey spent packing his clothes and calling around town for a place to stay. Finally, he found an old army buddy who was advertising for a roommate. That evening around six, Joey kissed the boys goodbye and started his new life as a single man living for Christ. In time, after prayerfully searching for a new church, Joey was led to a new congregation that had just formed. They were looking for someone like Joey who was willing to dedicate as much time to the ministry as possible.

Three years went by since Diana asked Joey to leave. Joey was now gainfully employed by the state department and answered his call into the ministry. He also served as founder and president of a teen outreach ministry that counseled teens rescued from abusive households.

Chapter 10

"When Evil Works for Good"

Joey was now in a position to help as many young people as he possibly could. One day, he received a call from community services needing his help for a mother and her two teenage children fleeing an abusive household. It was on a Friday evening and Joey had just gotten home after picking up his two boys for a weekend visit. The boys were anxious to spend every moment with their dad so they asked if they could tag along.

The drive to the shelter took about twenty minutes. Finally arriving there, Joey parked and rushed into the shelter. Upon entering the lobby, he noticed two kids sleeping on the couch. Before he reached the receptionist, a case worker came out to meet him.

"Reverend? Are you Reverend Denison?"

"Yes, I am he."

"I am Mrs. Jones, the case worker for tonight. Sorry we had to call at such a short notice, but we have this mother and her two kids who were badly abused by an alcoholic husband."

"Are those the kids sitting on the couch?" Joey asked the caseworker.

"Yes they are. The mother is in with the nurse getting bandaged up. It seems as though whenever her husband drinks, he becomes violent. Sometimes he beats her and then sometimes he beats the kids…oh, here she is now--Ms. Harris, I'd like you to meet Rev. Denison. He's the minister whom I felt would be good for you and the children to sit down and talk with."

"Hi…nice to meet you," said the woman with bruises on her face.

"Mrs. Jones, may we use one of the empty offices?" Joey asked.

"Oh sure. You're welcome to use this office right here."

"Thanks."

"Deneen and Cordell, y'all come on in here with us."

The two abused kids follow their mother and Joey into the office.

"Alright, Ms. Harris, the first thing I want to do is get a little information such as full names of every one in the family including your husband's full name. Let's start with your full name."

"Oh…yes sir. My full name is Gloria Harris. When my husband and I married I made the decision to hold on to my maiden name."

"Alright Ms. Harris, what are full names of your two children?" Joey asked.

"Cordell and Deneen Denison are their names."

"Denison?" Joey thought to himself. "What a coincidence that their last name is the same as mine. Who knows? We might be related."

"Two last questions," Joey said. "What is the name and address of your husband?"

"Well, his name is Claude Denison, and the address is…what's the matter, Rev'? You look as if you have seen a ghost."

"Well Ms. Harris, I'm having a shock attack at all of the information that you are giving me."

"What do you mean?" asked Ms. Harris.

"Well, first it was your kids' last name and now it's your husband's full name that is surprising me. You see, I have a brother that I have not seen in over ten years. Your husband has the same name as my brother's name. My next question is his age. How old is your husband?"

"My husband is about thirty-two years old…is your brother thirty-two as well?"

"You're exactly right," Joey said. "My brother is the same age."

The interview with Gloria Harris and her two children turned out to be quite emotional. As it turned out, this abused family was the family of his brother whom Joey had not seen in ten years. Once it was established that the two kids were actually Joey's niece and nephew that he had never met, he broke down and wept. The remainder of the interview was spent discussing the history of Claude's alcoholic addiction and the abuse inflicted upon his family. Gloria and the kids were given refuge in the shelter. Joey was so involved in the interview process that he almost forgot about his own two kids waiting in the lobby for him. He went out to get his two boys and introduced them to their new relatives. The night turned out to be an un-orchestrated family reunion.

The four kids hit it off right away. They exchanged telephone numbers and talked about getting together to spend some time at Joey's house in two weeks. The next day Joey made several phone calls in an attempt to contact his long lost brother. After he could not reach him by phone, he decided to take a drive down into the city to pay him a surprise visit. The kids had already gotten permission to spend the day with their aunt's kids who lived not far from where Joey lived, so he did not have to worry about finding a sitter for them.

On his way down to visit his brother, Joey dropped the kids off. After a twenty minute drive, he arrived at the housing project where his brother was supposed to be living. Sersum Heights was familiar grounds for Joey. Many of his classmates were raised in this housing project, which was only two blocks from where he was raised. It was a twenty-story high rise complex and his brother lived on the top floor. So while on the elevator, Joey had time to become seriously nervous about what could possibly take place during this visit. Nonetheless, he found himself standing at the apartment door. He took a deep breath, and then began knocking.
Joey knocked and waited.
He knocked and waited.

After he had concluded that his brother was not home, he turned and headed towards the elevator. Suddenly, he heard a door open and a raspy voice called out, "Can I help you?"

Joey turned around and glanced into the face of a tall, slender man with a balding head--a burning cigarette hanging from the side of his mouth. Joey was speechless.

Again the raspy voice called out, "*Can* I help you???"

Snapping out of his moment of shock, Joey finally spoke up. "Good morning, are you Claude Denison?"

"I am Claude. Who wants to know?"

"Listen man, I apologize for the inconvenience. I'm a minister from Prince William who..."

"...I'm not interested. Thank you for stopping by."

As he attempted to stumble back into the apartment, Joey called out his name. "Claude, it's me! Joey! Your brother!"

Claude, in his hung over state turned around and took a serious look at Joey's face. Suddenly, tears began to fall from his face as he cried out "Joey...man is that really you?"

Joey stepped forward and responded through the tears falling down his face, "Claude, it is really me."

After a time of renewal and obvious reconciliation, Claude extended an invitation for Joey to come inside. "Come on in man and don't look at the mess. You know I still remember what a clean freak you used to be. And judging from the way you are dressed, you still are. So what's up man, how did you find...no better still...what made you look for me? And what is this I heard you say about being a minister?"

"Too many questions at one time," Joey said. "But yes, I am a minister. And not just a minister, but a born-again Christian."

"So how did you end up getting all religious? I don't remember mom ever taking us to church, except it was for a funeral," Claude said.

"Well, give me chance to start from the beginning," Joey replied.

47

"Oh, I'm sorry man…have a seat. Can I get you something to drink?"

Claude stumbled his way into the kitchen. He looked into the refrigerator, and said, "What do you know? I got some water and half of a coke. Which will it be?"

"Claude, don't worry about it man, I don't want anything. Let's just talk," Joey said. "I am a minister and I am in charge of a special ministry that gives services to teenagers from broken and/or abusive families. We offer counseling, job placement and we also help find foster homes for them in cases where they have been abandoned…"

"Yeah man. I hear all of that, but you still have not answered my question. How did you become a minister? How long have you been this 'born again Christian' or whatever you call yourself?" said Claude.

"Well do you remember that I dropped out of high school in the eleventh grade and enlisted into the army? It was during my last two years in service, while stationed at Fort A.P. Hill; I met and married my wife who was a Christian woman. It was my wife who led me to Christ."

"Man, you got married??? I don't believe *this*. My little brother got himself a wife!" Claude shouted out. "Why didn't you bring her with you so that I could meet her…man, this is something!"

"Well it's not that easy," Joey said. "We have been divorced for three years now. I struggled for a while until God blessed me with a great career and ministry. So I bought a new house out in the suburbs in a place called South Haven."

"You know, I'm married also. And I got two beautiful kids. They are not here right now."

"Yes, I know," explained Joey. "As a matter of fact to make a long story short, it was through your wife that I found out how to get in touch with you."

"Oh…oh, hell no!" Claude said. "So WHERE is my family?"

"Listen Claude…where they are is not important right now--Just know that they are safe. She *did* talk to me about your drinking problem and I am here to help you get back on your feet. Claude…I am here to help you *however* I can."

Claude dropped his head and began to cry again. He said to Joey, "Man, I just can't believe you would stoop to help somebody like…*me*."

Joey replied, "But Claude…you are my brother. Why *wouldn't* I help you?"

"Well, you know man…we didn't treat you very good growing up. I don't know what it was, but we were wrong. I am *so* sorry for all that we put you through. Do you think…you could ever find it in your heart to forgive us?"

"Man, don't worry yourself about what happened. I <u>forgive</u> you. Anyway, the wrong that y'all did, God meant it for my good. So today is a new day—Now, I am not going to leave here until you let me get you some help for this drinking problem, but Claude, I can't help you unless you admit you need help."

Wiping his eyes as he looked into Joey's face, Claude confessed, "I do need help, man."

"Well, let's start by getting you cleaned up. Do you have clean slacks or jeans that you can put on?"

"Yeah, my wife did laundry before she left. My jeans are still in the laundry basket," Claude said.

"Well, while you are in the shower, I'll get you some clothes together."

After calling around town, Joey finally found a treatment center that would take in clients upon filling out paperwork for entrance into their program. The Harbor House was a new facility, supported by the Salvation Army and it was a good place for Claude to get a new start. The program at Harbor House was a six-month residential clinical program that also included classes for family resolution issues. Claude was willing and ready to at least give the staff at Harbor House a chance to help him overcome his alcohol addiction and abusive behavior. As for Claude's wife and two children, they remained living in the shelter while Gloria worked and saved enough money to lease an apartment. The shelter helped out as much as was allowed.

Chapter 11

"When Enemies Come for Help"

Joey finding his brother Claude led to the whereabouts of Junior and Michael. George, his oldest brother had left home at an early age. George would visit the family once a year during the Christmas holiday. He was an alcoholic as well, but with more control than the others.

Visitation at Harbor House was on Saturday and Sundays. While visiting with Claude one Saturday, Joey was surprised when both of his other two brothers, Junior and Michael, stopped by to visit Claude for the first time. Before the visit was over, both of them had apologized for their childhood rivalry acts of hatred. They all exchanged phone numbers, talked about old times and then went their separate ways vowing to stay in touch with each other. Joey always remained in contact with his mother and sister.

In talking with his brothers at Harbor House, Joey was able to discern that Michael and Junior both were seriously addicted to cocaine. Both became addicted after years of experimenting with marijuana. Over the course of the following year, Joey was called to rescue each one of his brothers. For Junior, he bailed him out twice with loans to pay for his rent that was in default. For Michael, it was once by his hospital bed after he had overdosed on a bad take of cocaine and once to bail him out of jail after being arrested for possession of an illegal substance. Each sacrifice that Joey made to help his own family opened other doors of ministry opportunity to help other families suffering with such things as substance abuse and spousal abuse as well as helping victims of childhood molestation.

It was the need for food during the time of a severe famine in the land that drew Joseph's brothers to Egypt. In Egypt, there was plenty of food. And Joseph was in charge of distributing this food. His days of completion and preparation for ministering to the needs of others had truly come in. This great story concludes with the completion and preparation of ministry for Joey Denison. And just like Joseph of the Bible, Joey's greatest opportunity and most effective time for ministry came when his brothers' need for help surfaced through a coincidental encounter with an abused sister-in-law.

Home is indeed the origin, the foundation of true ministry.